JAMAICA BAY SPECIES

JAMAICA BAY PAMPHLET LIBRARY 02

JAMAICA BAY SPECIES

STRUCTURES OF COASTAL RESILIENCE
Jamaica Bay Team
Spitzer School of Architecture
The City College of New York

Catherine Seavitt Nordenson, editor
Associate Professor of Landscape Architecture

Kjirsten Alexander
Research Associate

Danae Alessi
Research Associate

Eli Sands
Research Assistant

JAMAICA BAY PAMPHLET LIBRARY
02 Jamaica Bay Species

ISBN 978-1-942900-02-3

COPYRIGHT

CONTACT

Catherine Seavitt Nordenson
cseavittnordenson@ccny.cuny.edu
www.structuresofcoastalresilience.org

SCR Jamaica Bay Team
The City College of New York
Spitzer School of Architecture
Program in Landscape Architecture, Room 2M24A
141 Convent Avenue New York, New York 10031

COVER

Ghost Crab
photo: Don Riepe

supported by

THE ROCKEFELLER FOUNDATION   SCR Structures of Coastal Resilience   CUNY The City University of New York   The City College of New York

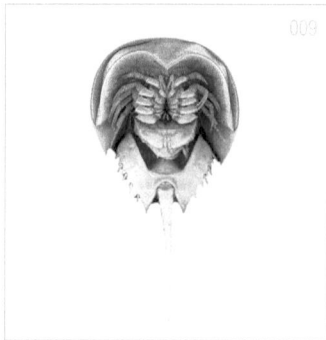

New York State Legal Status

● Endangered Species
● Threatened Species
● Special Concern Species
● Protected Wildlife
● Unprotected Wildlife
● Game
○ Classification Unknown

Invertebrates	Crustacea:	001	○	Blue Crab *(Callinectes sapidus)*
		002	○	Ghost Crab *(Ocypode quadrata)*
		003	○	American Lobster *(Homarus americanus)*
	Insecta:	004	●	Appalachian Azure *(Celastrina neglectamajor)*
		005	●	Checkered White *(Pieris protodice)*
		006	●	Salt Marsh Skipper *(Panoquina panoquin)*
		007	●	Tawny Emperor *(Asterocampa clyton)*
		008	●	White M Hairstreak *(Parrhasius m-album)*
	Merostomata:	009	○	Horseshoe Crab *(Limulus polyphemus)*
	Mollusca:	010	○	Atlantic Surfclam *(Spisula solidissima)*
		011	○	Blue Mussel *(Mytilus edulis)*
		012	○	Dwarf Surfclam *(Mulinia lateralis)*
		013	○	Northern Quahog *(Mercenaria mercenaria)*
		014	○	Softshell Clam *(Mya arenaria)*
Vertebrates	Amphibians:	015	◑	Eastern Spadefoot *(Scaphiopus h. holbrookii)*
		016	◑	Spotted Salamander *(Ambystoma maculatum)*

New York State Legal Status

- 🔴 Endangered Species
- 🔴 Threatened Species
- 🟢 Special Concern Species
- 🟢 Protected Wildlife
- 🔵 Unprotected Wildlife
- ⚪ Game
- ⚪ Classification Unknown

Birds: 017 American Bittern *(Botaurus lentiginosus)*
         018 American Black Duck *(Anas rubripes)**
         019 American Coot *(Fulica americana)**
         020 American Crow *(Corvus brachyrhynchos)**
         021 American Golden-Plover *(Pluvialis dominica)*
         022 American Goldfinch *(Spinus tristis)*
         023 American Kestrel *(Falco sparverius)*
         024 American Oystercatcher *(Haematopus palliatus)*
         025 American Redstart *(Setophaga ruticilla)*
         026 American Robin *(Turdus migratorius)*
         027 American Wigeon *(Anas americana)**
         028 American Woodcock *(Scolopax minor)**
         029 Atlantic Brant *(Branta bernicla)**
         030 Bank Swallow *(Riparia riparia)*
         031 Barn Owl *(Tyto alba)*
         032 Barn Swallow *(Hirundo rustica)*

New York State Legal Status

● Endangered Species
● Threatened Species
● Special Concern Species
● Protected Wildlife
● Unprotected Wildlife
● Game
○ Classification Unknown

Birds:	033	●	Belted Kingfisher *(Megaceryle alcyon)*
	034	●	Black-and-white Warbler *(Mniotilta varia)*
	035	●	Black Rail *(Laterallus jamaicensis)*
	036	◗	Black Skimmer *(Rynchops niger)*
	037	●	Black-bellied Plover *(Pluvialis squatarola)*
	038	●	Black-billed Cuckoo *(Coccyzus erythropthalmus)*
	039	●	Blackburnian Warbler *(Dendroica fusca)*
	040	●	Black-capped Chickadee *(Poecile atricapillus)*
	041	●	Black-crowned Night Heron *(Nycticorax nycticorax)*
	042	●	Blackpoll Warbler *(Dendroica striata)*
	043	●	Black-throated Blue Warbler *(Dendroica caerulescens)*
	044	●	Black-throated Green Warbler *(Dendroica virens)*
	045	●	Blue Jay *(Cyanocitta cristata)*
	046	●	Blue-gray Gnatcatcher *(Polioptila caerulea)*
	047	●	Blue-winged Teal *(Anas discors)**
	048	●	Boat-tailed Grackle *(Quiscalus major)*

049

050

051

052

053

054

055

056

057

058

059

060

061

062

063

064

New York State Legal Status

- 🔴 Endangered Species
- 🔴 Threatened Species
- 🟢 Special Concern Species
- 🟢 Protected Wildlife
- 🔵 Unprotected Wildlife
- ⚪ Game
- ⚪ Classification Unknown

Birds:	049	🟢	Bobolink *(Dolichonyx oryzivorus)*
	050	🟢	Bonaparte's Gull *(Larus philadelphia)*
	051	🟢	Brown Thrasher *(Toxostoma rufum)*
	052	🟢	Brown-headed Cowbird *(Molothrus ater)*
	053	⚪	Bufflehead *(Bucephala albeola)**
	054	⚪	Canada Goose *(Branta canadensis)**
	055	🟢	Canada Warbler *(Cardellina canadensis)*
	056	⚪	Canvasback *(Aythya valisineria)**
	057	🟢	Cattle Egret *(Bubulcus ibis)*
	058	🟢	Cedar Waxwing *(Bombycilla cedrorum)*
	059	🟢	Chestnut-sided Warbler *(Dendroica pensylvanica)*
	060	🟢	Chimney Swift *(Chaetura pelagica)*
	061	🟢	Chipping Sparrow *(Spizella passerina)*
	062	🟢	Clapper Rail *(Rallus longirostris)*
	063	⚪	Common Goldeneye *(Bucephala clangula)**
	064	🟢	Common Grackle *(Quiscalus quiscula)*

New York State Legal Status

● Endangered Species
● Threatened Species
● Special Concern Species
● Protected Wildlife
● Unprotected Wildlife
● Game
○ Classification Unknown

Birds: 065 ◗ Common Loon *(Gavia immer)*
066 ● Common Moorhen *(Gallinula galeata)*
067 ● Common Tern *(Sterna hirundo)*
068 ● Common Yellowthroat *(Geothlypis trichas)*
069 ◗ Cooper's Hawk *(Accipiter cooperii)*
070 ● Dark-eyed Junco *(Junco hyemalis)*
071 ● Double-crested Cormorant *(Phalacrocorax auritus)*
072 ● Downy Woodpecker *(Picoides pubescens)*
073 ● Dunlin *(Calidris alpina)*
074 ● Eastern Kingbird *(Tyrannus tyrannus)*
075 ● Eastern Meadowlark *(Sturnella magna)*
076 ● Eastern Towhee *(Pipilo erythrophthalmus)*
077 ● Eastern Wood-pewee *(Contopus virens)*
078 ● European Starling *(Sturnus vulgaris)*
079 ● Field Sparrow *(Spizella pusilla)*
080 ● Fish Crow *(Corvus ossifragus)*

081

082

083

084

085

086

087

088

089

090

091

092

093

094

095

096

New York State Legal Status

● Endangered Species
● Threatened Species
● Special Concern Species
● Protected Wildlife
● Unprotected Wildlife
● Game
○ Classification Unknown

Birds: 081 ● Forster's Tern *(Sterna forsteri)*
        082 ● Gadwall *(Anas strepera)**
        083 ● Glossy Ibis *(Plegadis falcinellus)*
        084 ◗ Grasshopper Sparrow *(Ammodramus savannarum)*
        085 ● Gray Catbird *(Dumetella carolinensis)*
        086 ● Great Black-backed Gull *(Larus marinus)*
        087 ● Great Blue Heron *(Ardea herodias)*
        088 ● Great Cormorant *(Phalacrocorax carbo)*
        089 ● Great Crested Flycatcher *(Myiarchus crinitus)*
        090 ● Great Egret *(Ardea alba)*
        091 ● Greater Scaup *(Aythya marila)**
        092 ● Green Heron *(Butorides virescens)*
        093 ● Green-winged Teal *(Anas crecca)**
        094 ● Gull-billed Tern *(Sterna nilotica)*
        095 ● Hairy Woodpecker *(Picoides villosus)*
        096 ● Hermit Thrush *(Catharus guttatus)*

 097

 098

 099

 100

 101

 102

 103

 104

 105

 106

 107

 108

 109

 110

 111

 112

New York State Legal Status

- ● Endangered Species
- ● Threatened Species
- ● Special Concern Species
- ● Protected Wildlife
- ● Unprotected Wildlife
- ● Game
- ○ Classification Unknown

Birds: 097 ● Herring Gull *(Larus argentatus)*
098 ● Hooded Merganser *(Lophodytes cucullatus)**
099 ● Horned Grebe *(Podiceps auritus)*
100 ◗ Horned Lark *(Eremophila alpestris)*
101 ● House Finch *(Haemorhous mexicanus)*
102 ● House Sparrow *(Passer domesticus)*
103 ● House Wren *(Troglodytes aedon)*
104 ● Killdeer *(Charadrius vociferus)*
105 ● Laughing Gull *(Leucophaeus atricilla)*
106 ● Least Bittern *(Ixobrychus exilis)*
107 ● Least Flycatcher *(Empidonax minimus)*
108 ● Least Sandpiper *(Calidris minutilla)*
109 ● Least Tern *(Sternula antillarum)*
110 ● Lesser Scaup *(Aythya affinis)**
111 ● Little Blue Heron *(Egretta caerulea)*
112 ● Long-eared Owl *(Asio otus)*

113

114

115

116

117

118

119

120

121

122

123

124

125

126

127

128

New York State Legal Status

● Endangered Species
● Threatened Species
● Special Concern Species
● Protected Wildlife
● Unprotected Wildlife
● Game
○ Classification Unknown

Birds:			
113	●	Magnolia Warbler	(Dendroica magnolia)
114	●	Mallard	(Anas platyrhynchos)*
115	●	Mallard x American Black Duck Hybrid	(Anas platyrhynchos x A. rubripes)*
116	●	Marsh Wren	(Cistothorus palustris)
117	●	Merlin	(Falco columbarius)
118	●	Mourning Dove	(Zenaida macroura)
119	●	Mute Swan	(Cygnus olor)
120	●	Northern Bobwhite	(Colinus virginianus)*
121	●	Northern Cardinal	(Cardinalis cardinalis)
122	●	Northern Flicker	(Colaptes auratus)
123	●	Northern Harrier	(Circus cyaneus)
124	●	Northern Mockingbird	(Mimus polyglottos)
125	●	Northern Oriole	(Icterus spurius)
126	●	Northern Parula	(Parula americana)
127	●	Northern Pintail	(Anas acuta)*
128	●	Northern Rough-winged Swallow	(Stelgidopteryx serripennis)

New York State Legal Status

● Endangered Species
● Threatened Species
● Special Concern Species
● Protected Wildlife
● Unprotected Wildlife
● Game
○ Classification Unknown

Birds: 129 ● Northern Shoveler *(Anas clypeata)**
        130 ● Northern Waterthrush *(Parkesia noveboracensis)*
        131 ● Osprey *(Pandion haliaetus)*
        132 ● Ovenbird *(Seiurus aurocapilla)*
        133 ● Palm Warbler *(Dendroica palmarum)*
        134 ● Peregrine Falcon *(Falco peregrinus)*
        135 ● Pied-billed Grebe *(Podilymbus podiceps)*
        136 ● Piping Plover *(Charadrius melodus)*
        137 ● Prairie Warbler *(Dendroica discolor)*
        138 ● Purple Finch *(Haemorhous purpureus)*
        139 ● Red Knot *(Calidris canutus)*
        140 ● Red-bellied Woodpecker *(Melanerpes carolinus)*
        141 ● Red-breasted Merganser *(Mergus serrator)**
        142 ● Red-eyed Vireo *(Vireo olivaceus)*
        143 ● Redhead *(Aythya americana)**
        144 ● Red-shouldered Hawk *(Buteo lineatus)*

145

146

147

148

149

150

151

152

153

154

155

156

157

158

159

160

New York State Legal Status

- 🔴 Endangered Species
- 🔴 Threatened Species
- 🟢 Special Concern Species
- 🟢 Protected Wildlife
- 🔵 Unprotected Wildlife
- ⚪ Game
- ⚪ Classification Unknown

Birds:
145	🟢	Red-tailed Hawk *(Buteo jamaicensis)*
146	🟢	Red-winged Blackbird *(Agelaius phoeniceus)*
147	⚪	Ring-necked Pheasant *(Phasianus colchicus)**
148	🔵	Rock Pigeon *(Columba livia)*
149	🔴	Roseate Tern *(Sterna dougallii)*
150	🟢	Rose-breasted Grosbeak *(Pheucticus ludovicianus)*
151	🟢	Rough-legged Hawk *(Buteo lagopus)*
152	🟢	Ruby-throated Hummingbird *(Archilochus colubris)*
153	⚪	Ruddy Duck *(Oxyura jamaicensis)**
154	🟢	Ruddy Turnstone *(Arenaria interpres)*
155	🟢	Saltmarsh Sparrow *(Ammodramus caudacutus)*
156	🟢	Sanderling *(Calidris alba)*
157	🟢	Savannah Sparrow *(Passerculus sandwichensis)*
158	🟢	Scarlet Tanager *(Piranga olivacea)*
159	🟢	Seaside Sparrow *(Ammodramus maritimus)*
160	🟢	Semipalmated Plover *(Charadrius semipalmatus)*

New York State Legal Status

- 🔴 Endangered Species
- 🔴 Threatened Species
- 🟢 Special Concern Species
- 🟢 Protected Wildlife
- 🔵 Unprotected Wildlife
- ⚪ Game
- ⚪ Classification Unknown

Birds:

161	🟢	Semipalmated Sandpiper *(Calidris pusilla)*
162	🟢	Sharp-shinned Hawk *(Accipiter striatus)*
163	🔴	Short-eared Owl *(Asio flammeus)*
164	⚪	Snow Goose *(Chen caerulescens)**
165	🟢	Snowy Egret *(Egretta thula)*
166	🟢	Song Sparrow *(Melospiza melodia)*
167	⚪	Sora *(Porzana carolina)**
168	🟢	Spotted Sandpiper *(Actitis macularius)*
169	🟢	Swainson's Thrush *(Catharus ustulatus)*
170	🟢	Swamp Sparrow *(Melospiza georgiana)*
171	🟢	Tree Swallow *(Tachycineta bicolor)*
172	🟢	Tricolored Heron *(Egretta tricolor)*
173	🟢	Tufted Titmouse *(Baeolophus bicolor)*
174	🔴	Upland Sandpiper *(Bartramia longicauda)*
175	🟢	Veery *(Catharus fuscescens)*
176	⚪	Virginia Rail *(Rallus limicola)**

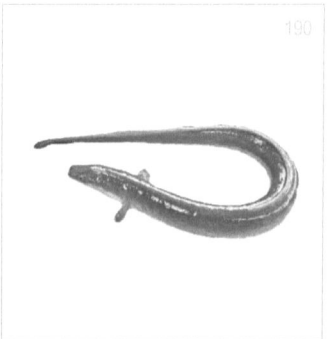

New York State Legal Status

- ● Endangered Species
- ● Threatened Species
- ● Special Concern Species
- ● Protected Wildlife
- ● Unprotected Wildlife
- ● Game
- ○ Classification Unknown

Birds:	177	●	Warbling Vireo *(Vireo gilvus)*
	178	●	White-eyed Vireo *(Vireo griseus)*
	179	●	White-rumped Sandpiper *(Calidris fuscicollis)*
	180	●	White-throated Sparrow *(Zonotrichia albicollis)*
	181	●	Willet *(Tringa semipalmata)*
	182	●	Willow Flycatcher *(Empidonax traillii)*
	183	●	Wood Duck *(Aix sponsa)**
	184	●	Wood Thrush *(Hylocichla mustelina)*
	185	●	Yellow Warbler *(Dendroica petechia)*
	186	●	Yellow-billed Cuckoo *(Coccyzus americanus)*
	187	●	Yellow-crowned Night Heron *(Nyctanassa violacea)*
	188	●	Yellow-rumped Warbler *(Dendroica coronata)*
Fish:	189	●	Alewife Herring *(Alosa pseudoharengus)*
	190	●	American Eel *(Anguilla rostrata)*
	191	●	American Sandlance *(Ammodytes americanus)*
	192	●	American Shad *(Alosa sapidissima)*

30

193

194

195

196

197

198

199

200

201

202

203

204

205

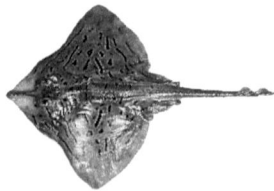

206

207

208

New York State Legal Status

● Endangered Species
● Threatened Species
● Special Concern Species
● Protected Wildlife
● Unprotected Wildlife
○ Game
○ Classification Unknown

Fish: 193 ● Atlantic Cod *(Gadus morhua)*
        194 ● Atlantic Herring *(Clupea harengus)*
        195 ● Atlantic Menhaden *(Brevoortia tyrannus)*
        196 ● Atlantic Needlefish *(Strongylura marina)*
        197 ● Atlantic Silverside *(Menidia menidia)*
        198 ● Atlantic Sturgeon *(Acipenser oxyrinchus)*
        199 ● Atlantic Tomcod *(Microgadus tomcod)*
        200 ● Banded Killifish *(Fundulus diaphanus)*
        201 ● Bay Anchovy *(Anchoa mitchilli)*
        202 ● Black Sea Bass *(Centropristis striata)*
        203 ● Blueback Herring *(Alosa aestivalis)*
        204 ● Bluefish *(Pomatomus saltatrix)*
        205 ● Butterfish *(Peprilus triacanthus)*
        206 ○ Clearnose skate *(Raja eglanteria)*
        207 ● Cunner *(Tautogolabrus adspersus)*
        208 ● Fourspine Stickleback *(Apeltes quadracus)*

New York State Legal Status

● Endangered Species
● Threatened Species
● Special Concern Species
● Protected Wildlife
● Unprotected Wildlife
● Game
○ Classification Unknown

Fish:
209	●	Grubby Sculpin	*(Myoxcephalus aenaeus)*
210	●	Hogchoker	*(Trinectes maculatus)*
211	●	Inland Silverside	*(Menidia beryllina)*
212	○	Little Skate	*(Raja erinacea)*
213	●	Mummichog	*(Fundulus heteroclitus)*
214	●	Naked Goby	*(Gobiosoma bosci)*
215	●	Northern Kingfish	*(Menticirrhus saxatilis)*
216	●	Northern Searobin	*(Prionotus carolinus)*
217	●	Northern Pipefish	*(Syngnathus fuscus)*
218	○	Oyster Toadfish	*(Opsanus tau)*
219	●	Red Hake	*(Urophycis chuss)*
220	●	Scup	*(Stenotomus chrysops)*
221	●	Seaboard Goby	*(Gobiosoma ginsburgi)*
222	●	Shortnose Sturgeon	*(Acipenser brevirostrum)*
223	●	Silver Hake	*(Merluccius bilinearis)*
224	●	Smooth Dogfish	*(Mustelus canis)*

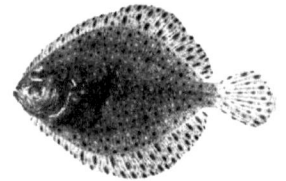

New York State Legal Status

● Endangered Species
● Threatened Species
● Special Concern Species
● Protected Wildlife
● Unprotected Wildlife
● Game
○ Classification Unknown

Fish: 225 ○ Spiny Dogfish *(Squalus acanthias)*
226 ● Spot *(Leiostomas xanthurus)*
227 ● Spotfin Killifish *(Fundulus luciae)*
228 ● Striped Bass *(Morone saxatilis)*
229 ● Striped Mullet *(Mugil cephalus)*
230 ● Striped Searobin *(Prionotus evolans)*
231 ● Summer Flounder *(Paralichthys dentatus)*
232 ● Tautog *(Tautoga onitis)*
233 ● Weakfish *(Cynoscion regalis)*
234 ○ White Hake *(Urophycis tenuis)*
235 ● White Perch *(Morone americana)*
236 ● Windowpane Flounder *(Scophthalmus aquosus)*
237 ● Winter Flounder *(Pleuronectes americanus)*
Mammals: 238 ● Bottlenose Dolphin *(Tursiops truncatus)*
239 ● Fin Whale *(Balaenoptera physalus)*
240 ● Harbor Seal *(Phoca vitulina)*

Sources:

New York City Audubon: Jamaica Bay Wildlife Refuge Restoration Recommendations for the West Pond
http://www.nycaudubon.org/images/pdf/Restoration_Recommendations_West_Pond_NYC_Audubon_02_24_14_web.pdf

National Oceanic and Atmospheric Administration: Environmental Sensitivity Index Maps
http://response.restoration.noaa.gov/maps-and-spatial-data/environmental-sensitivity-index-esi-maps.html

U.S. Fish and Wildlife Service: Jamaica Bay and Breezy Point List of Species of Special Emphasis
http://nctc.fws.gov/resources/knowledge-resources/pubs5/web_link/tables/jba_tab.htm

USDA, APHIS, Wildlife Services: Bird Hazard Reduction Program - John F. Kennedy International Airport
http://www.aphis.usda.gov/regulations/ws/ws_new_york_jfk_2.shtml

*Game designation is per New York State legal status however hunting is prohibited in all areas of the
Gateway National Recreation Area Jamaica Bay Unit
http://www.nps.gov/gate/parkmgmt/upload/2013-GATE-Compendium-Final.pdf

New York State Legal Status

- 🔴 Endangered Species
- 🔴 Threatened Species
- 🟢 Special Concern Species
- 🟢 Protected Wildlife
- 🔵 Unprotected Wildlife
- ⚪ Game
- ⚪ Classification Unknown

Mammals:	241	🔴	Humpback Whale *(Megaptera novaeangliae)*
	242	🔴	Northern Right Whale *(Eubalaena glacialis)*
	243	🔴	Sperm Whale *(Physeter catodon)*
Reptiles:	244	🟢	Eastern Box Turtle *(Terrapene c. carolina)*
	245	🔴	Kemp's Ridley Sea Turtle *(Lepidochelys kempii)*
	246	🔴	Leatherback Sea Turtle *(Dermochelys coriacea)*
	247	🔴	Loggerhead Sea Turtle *(Caretta caretta)*
	248	◑	Northern Diamondback Terrapin *(Malaclemys t. terrapin)*

www.ingramcontent.com/pod-product-compliance
Lightning Source LLC
Chambersburg PA
CBHW060826270326
41931CB00002B/74